Contents

Any words appearing in the text in bold, **like this**, are explained in the Glossary. You can also look out for them in the Star words box at the bottom of each page.

One of a kind

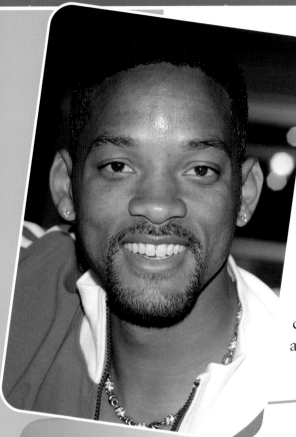

Every entertainer wants to be the best in the business. Will Smith has been the best three times. He has become a star in music, television and films. Few people Will's age have done this.

Music man

Will was a star when he was a teenager. He was a success in the early days of rap music. He and his friend, Jeff Townes, called themselves DJ Jazzy Jeff and the Fresh Prince.

ALL ABOUT WILL

Full name: Willard C. Smith Jr
Born: 25 September 1968
Place of birth: West Philadelphia, Pennsylvania, USA
Family: Willard Sr and Caroline (parents); Harry, Pamela and Ellen (brother and sisters)
Height: 6′ 2″ (1.88 metres)
Married: Sheree Zampino (1992); Jada Pinkett (1997)
Children: Trey, Jaden and Willow
First album: *Rock the House* (1987)
First television series: *The Fresh Prince of Bel Air*
First major film: *Bad Boys* (1995)
Other interests: Plays golf and chess; speaks fluent Spanish; owns Overbrook Entertainment

Star words   professional someone who does their job very well

STAR ★ FILES

Will Smith

Mark Stewart

www.raintreepublishers.co.uk

Visit our website to find out more information about **Raintree** books.

To order:

 Phone 44 (0) 1865 888113

 Send a fax to 44 (0) 1865 314091

Visit the Raintree Bookshop at **www.raintreepublishers.co.uk** to browse our catalogue and order online.

 Produced for Raintree by
White-Thomson Publishing Ltd
Bridgewater Business Centre
210 High Street, Lewes, BN7 2NH

First published in Great Britain by Raintree,
Halley Court, Jordan Hill, Oxford OX2 8EJ,
part of Harcourt Education.
Raintree is a registered trademark of Harcourt
Education Ltd.

© Harcourt Education Ltd 2005
First published in paperback in 2005
The moral right of the proprietor has
been asserted.

Editorial: Nick Hunter and Catherine Clarke
Design: Leishman Design and Michelle Lisseter
Picture Research: Nicola Hodgson
Production: Kevin Blackman
Project Management: Nicola Hodgson

Originated by Dot Gradations Ltd
Printed and bound in China by South China
Printing Company

ISBN 1 844 43832 5 (hardback)
09 08 07 06 05
10 9 8 7 6 5 4 3 2 1

ISBN 1 844 43839 2 (paperback)
10 09 08 07 06 05
10 9 8 7 6 5 4 3 2 1

**British Library Cataloguing in
Publication Data**
Stewart, Mark
Will Smith. – (Star Files)
791.4' 3028' 092
A full catalogue record for this book is
available from the British Library.

Acknowledgements
The publishers would like to thank the
following for permission to reproduce
photographs: Allstar Picture Library pp. **12–13**,
14, **17** (l), **18**, **21** (l), **21** (r), **24** (r), **27** (l), **33**,
41 (r), **42**, **43** (l); Corbis pp. **6** (l), **7**, **8**, **17** (r),
31 (l); Retna Pictures pp. **5**, **6** (r), **9**, **10** (r), **12**
(l), **13**, **23** (r), **30**, **31** (r), **35** (b), **37** (l), **40**; Rex
Features pp. **10** (l), **11**, **15** (l), **15** (r), **16**, **19** (l)
19 (r), **20** (l), **20** (r), **22**, **23** (l), **24** (l), **25**, **26**,
27 (r), **28**, **29** (t), **29** (b), **32** (l), **32** (r), **34**, **35**
(t), **36**, **37** (r), **38**, **39** (l), **39** (r), **41** (l), **43**.
Cover photograph reproduced with permission
of Rex Features.

Quote sources p. **14** *Newsday*, 2 April 1995,
p. **34** *Arizona Reporter*, 3 January 2002. All
other quotes from Internet Movie Database.

The publishers would like to thank Voirrey
Carr and Simone Apel for their assistance in
the preparation of this book.

They sold millions of albums and won many awards. Will went on to star in the television show *The Fresh Prince of Bel Air*. Since then, he has made many major films.

Making choices

Will has worked hard to become a good rapper and actor. He has taken risks and made hard choices. Sometimes Will made the right choices, and sometimes he did not. He turned down some good film **roles** because he wanted better ones. In his twenties, Will spent too much time on his career and not enough on his family. He paid a heavy price for this mistake.

Will power

Will is a true **professional**. He is serious about his work. He always wants to improve. Will's fans love to watch him perform. His fellow professionals say that Will is great to work with.

Will is a great performer to watch.

Find out later

What sitcom did Will appear on for six years?

Which **role** won Will an Academy Award **nomination** for Best Actor?

Who convinced Will to appear in the hit film *Men in Black*?

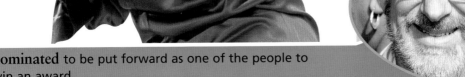

Starting out

Will was brought up in Philadelphia, USA. This is where he first got into music and acting.

Will's parents are called Willard and Caroline Smith. Will was one of four children. The family lived in West Philadelphia. Will's dad owned a refrigeration company. His mum worked as an **administrator** at a local school. Will was named Willard Jr, but people called him 'Will'. The Smith children liked to have fun. They also knew how important it was to work hard. Their parents made sure they did their homework every night and helped them study for tests.

Overbrook achievers

Will went to Overbrook High School in his home city of Philadelphia, USA. Many well-known athletes and musicians also went there, including US basketball hero Wilt Chamberlain.

Will with his dad and his sons Trey and Jaden.

Star words administrator someone who helps to run a school, business or other organization

Prince charming

Will did well in school. He liked maths and science best. Will had a good sense of humour and was the class clown. Sometimes teachers got angry with him for being too silly. Will could always talk his way out of trouble, however. The other children called him 'Prince' because he could be so charming.

Rap lover

Will became a fan of rap music when he was young. He bought his first rap record when he was twelve and soon had a large record collection. He memorized the words and copied the different rapping styles. He was also a DJ at local parties.

Allen Iverson plays for the Philadelphia 76ers, Will's favourite basketball team.

Signature style

Will used his love of music and his fun personality to develop a new rapping style. By the time he was fourteen, a lot of people in Philadelphia were talking about him. Will started taking acting classes at high school. This made him want to perform on stage. In 1985, Will met Jeff Townes at a party in Will's neighbourhood. Jeff was a few years older than Will. He was one of the top DJs in Philadelphia. Will asked if he could rap with him at the party. For the next few hours they performed together. They were very good. People were amazed that they had just met that day.

76ers

Will's favourite sport when he was young was basketball. He liked to play, and he loved to watch his local team, the Philadelphia 76ers.

Educated decision

Will did well in school. His grades were good enough for him to get into almost any college in the country. Going to college would mean giving up his music career, though. Will told his parents he wanted to be a rapper. They said it would be okay to try it for a year.

The Fresh Prince

Will and Jeff began playing together at parties when Will was fifteen. They were called DJ Jazzy Jeff and the Fresh Prince. Will would also go to Jeff's house after school and at the weekends. Jeff had turned his basement into a recording studio. They would write songs together. They recorded their best songs on a tape. They gave the tape to Dana Goodman. Dana was a record **producer** in Philadelphia.

Big break

Dana Goodman was impressed with the tape and signed up Will and Jeff to make a record. Their first single was a song called 'Girls ain't nothing but trouble'. It was a big hit in the USA and the UK. Jive Records signed up Will and Jeff to do a whole album. This was called *Rock the House*.

DJ Jazzy Jeff and the Fresh Prince.

Star words   producer person in charge of making a record, film or television show

Grandmaster Flash and the Furious Five were among the first stars of rap music.

The early days of rap

Rap music had only been going for ten years when Will came along. It began on street corners and in playgrounds in New York during the 1970s. Will began listening to rap around 1980. One of the songs that **inspired** Will was 'The message', by Grandmaster Flash and the Furious Five.

It sold more than 500,000 copies. Will had his first show business success. He was still only seventeen years old.

Rise to fame

Will and Jeff were on their way. Within a year, they were on tour with rap superstars LL Cool J and Public Enemy. In 1988, they released their second album. It was called *He's the DJ, I'm the Rapper*. They had a huge hit with their song 'Parents just don't understand'.

★ Star fact

To this day, Will has a simple rule: if his mother cannot watch it or listen to it, he will not perform it. Will wants to tell stories that make people think a little, smile a little, and most of all have fun.

inspire give someone the idea or motivation to do something

Will and Jeff at the Grammy awards in 1991.

Rapper's roots

DJ Jazzy Jeff and the Fresh Prince had a lot of success. They had their critics too, though. Other rappers said they were too soft. Will wrote songs about the passion, humour and **anxiety** in the lives of young people. Other rappers wrote about gangs and the dangers of life on the streets. They said Will and Jeff made music for white people because they ignored the **hardships** and **injustice** suffered by African Americans. They said that Will was a fake.

★ ★ ★ ★ ★ ★ ★ ★ ★ ★

Grammy time

DJ Jazzy Jeff and the Fresh Prince won the first-ever Grammy award for a rap single in 1988. They won a second Grammy in 1991 for their song 'Summertime'.

★ ★ ★ ★ ★ ★ ★ ★ ★ ★

Will's rapping was completely different from the more serious style of rap groups like Public Enemy.

10

True to life

Will defended himself. He said that he wrote about the things in his life. Most rap fans did not live among murderers and drug dealers, and neither did he. If he wrote about things he did not understand, that would make him a fake.

Grammy goof

Will's career was on the rise in 1988. In that year, 'Parents just don't understand' won the first-ever **Grammy** award for Best Rap Single. When Will and Jeff got the news, they were very happy. Then they were told they would not be on television. Rap was not 'big enough' yet. This made them angry. They decided not to accept the award. Just one year later, rap artists were a major part of the Grammys. Since then, rap and hip-hop have come to be among the most important and popular types of modern music.

Chance meeting

Will's chance to be on television came when he met a record **producer** called Benny Medina. Benny was an **orphan** who had grown up with **foster families**. He spent many years living in dangerous neighbourhoods. Benny's last foster family was very wealthy, however. They lived in Beverly Hills, California. Benny thought his story might make a good television show. Will would be just the right person to play the main character.

The sound of Philadelphia

Long before Will, Philadelphia was famous for its musicians. These include:
- blues legend Bessie Smith
- opera singer Marian Anderson
- rock 'n' roll singers Bill Haley and Chubby Checker (above)
- R 'n' B stars The Stylistics
- rock duo Hall and Oates
- pop star Patti LaBelle.

injustice unfairness
orphan someone whose parents are dead

The Fresh Prince of Bel Air

Benny and Will wanted to turn their idea for a comedy show into a reality. They asked their friend Quincy Jones to help them. He liked the idea. Quincy called people he knew at a US television station. They liked the idea too. They agreed to let Will **audition**. He was very good. He seemed to be a natural actor. The station gave the show the go-ahead. It was called *The Fresh Prince of Bel Air*.

> " I was trying so hard. I would memorize the entire script. "

Will and Jeff stayed friends when Will became a television star.

Still friends

The more time Will gave to acting, the less time he had for music. Many fans thought he would break up with Jeff Townes. They remained friends, though, and Will created a part for Jeff on *The Fresh Prince of Bel Air*.

Star words

audition interview for a musician or actor, where they show their skills

Totally fresh

The first episode was shown on 10 September 1990. Will played a **wise-cracking** teenager from Philadelphia. His mother sends him to live with his wealthy aunt and uncle in their California mansion. The show was about how Will dealt with his change of lifestyle. He was charming and funny. Audiences loved him. The show was a hit. It ran on US television until 1996.

Learning to act

Will worried that the other actors on the show would be unhappy that he was playing the lead. After all, he had done very little acting before.

They saw how much talent Will had, however. They also saw how hard he worked to improve. They were happy to help Will in any way they could. *Fresh Prince* was a comedy, but Will thought he might want to play a serious part one day. He often asked his **co-stars** (and the show's guest stars) how they handled different acting challenges.

Will and some of his co-stars in a scene from *The Fresh Prince of Bel Air*.

Will often worried about making his acting better.

Serious side

When Will started on *Fresh Prince*, he was scared of forgetting his lines. He would sometimes 'freeze up'. Sometimes he even shouted out the other actors' lines. Will became a better actor when he started to explore the characters he played. Once he understood a part, he could relax. He could concentrate on the details that make a great performance.

First films

Oscar link

In *Six Degrees of Separation*, Will played a young man who pretends to be Sidney Poitier's son. Poitier is a famous actor. He was the first African American actor to win an Oscar. He received another Oscar in 2002 for lifetime achievement. That year another African American was **nominated** for Best Actor – Will Smith, for his role in *Ali*.

Back in 1986, Will had a very small **role** in a film called *The Imagemaker*. He loved the experience. He hoped he would get another chance to act. Will's success on *Fresh Prince* soon led to more film roles. His first big role was in the 1992 film *Where the Day Takes You*. Will played a young boy named Manny. This role helped to prove that Will could be a serious actor.

> A rapper is about being completely true to yourself. Being an actor is about changing who you are.

Will in the comedy *Made in America*.

Star words

con man someone who wins the trust of others, then steals from them

Made in America

Will also had a part in the comedy film *Made in America*. This starred Whoopi Goldberg and Ted Danson. Will's fans hoped to see him in more films. They probably never expected to see him in a film like *Six Degrees of Separation*, though.

Will in *Six Degrees of Separation*.

Breakthrough role

Six Degrees of Separation was a small, **low budget** film. Will played the role of Paul. Paul is a **con man** who takes advantage of a rich couple. It was a serious and complicated part. Film critics praised Will's acting. This made Will very proud. He had worked hard to play a character who was nothing like him. The film gave him the confidence to play any part.

Stockard Channing starred with Will in *Six Degrees of Separation*.

Will's fan

Six Degrees of Separation was directed by Fred Schepisi. Fred became a big fan of Will. Will's **co-star** in the film, Stockard Channing, was nominated for an Academy Award. Fred told everyone that Will should have been nominated, too.

---

low budget small amount of money available to spend. A low budget film does not cost much money to make.

★ ★ ★ ★ ★ ★ ★ ★ ★ ★

Co-stars

You can judge a young actor by the quality of the actors who agree to co-star with him. In Will's case the list is impressive. It includes Tommy Lee Jones, Kevin Kline, Jeff Goldblum, Gene Hackman and Donald Sutherland.

★ ★ ★ ★ ★ ★ ★ ★ ★ ★

Star quality

What makes a film star? Will often asked himself this question. He knew that the best actors made you believe that the people they played were real. They could be funny, serious, sad, energetic, gentle or dangerous during the same film.

The right roles

Will believed that he could act all of these emotions. Now he had to look for parts that would let him prove it. This was not easy. Most people still knew him as a rapper and television comedy star. The film **roles** he wanted were out there, but they were not being offered to him.

Proving himself

Before Will could pick and choose his roles, he had to prove that his fans would pay to watch him on the **silver screen**. His best chance to prove this would be in an action film. Will had the good looks, strength and **charisma** needed to star in this type of film. He waited for a role that would let him show off his serious side as well as his sense of humour. He did not have to wait long.

> Jeff Goldblum starred with Will in *Independence Day*.

Star words

silver screen nickname for the large screen at the cinema
charisma charm and appeal

Bad Boys

Will got his first chance to star in a film in the 1995 hit *Bad Boys*. His **co-star** was Martin Lawrence. Martin was a comedian who also had a successful television show. *Bad Boys* was about two police officers protecting an important **witness**. It mixed action with comedy. Will played his part with just the right amount of each. *Bad Boys* was very successful. It made more than US$100 million. This proved that Will's star power could draw a big audience.

Rising salary

Will was paid US$50,000 for his work on *Where the Day Takes You* in 1992. Ten years later, he earned US$20 million for *Men in Black II*.

Bad Boys was Will's first action film.

witness someone who has seen a crime take place

Model hero

Will says that he based the character he played in *Independence Day* on Han Solo in the *Star Wars* films. Han Solo was played by Harrison Ford, who is one of Will's screen heroes.

★ ★ ★ ★ ★ ★ ★ ★ ★ ★ ★

Han Solo **inspired** Will's role in *Independence Day*.

Action hero

After the success of *Bad Boys*, Will seemed the perfect choice to appear in the film *Independence Day*. This was a **big-budget** science-fiction film with lots of special effects. The **producers** of the film wanted to be sure that people would go to see it. Will played the part of a fighter pilot. He helps to stop aliens invading the planet. Will was tough, sensitive and funny.

Preparing for roles

Will has had to do some unusual things to prepare for his film parts. He worked for several weeks with fighter pilots so he could be more realistic in *Independence Day*.

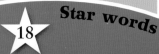

Star words

big budget large amount of money available to spend.
A big budget film is made using a lot of money.

For *Bad Boys* (and *Bad Boys II*) he had to learn about how police officers work. He also had to learn how to handle a gun. For *Men in Black* (and *Men in Black II*), he had to act with aliens. This was difficult because they were not really on the **set**. The aliens were added later with computers. Sometimes Will had to do his scenes talking to a ball on the end of a stick!

Trey Smith is Will's eldest son.

Will played a fighter pilot in *Independence Day*.

First child

In 1991, Will met a young woman named Sheree Zampino. They were married the following spring and had a son, Trey. The marriage ended in 1995 and Will's song 'Just the two of us' was written for Trey.

set part of a film studio where a film is shot

Aliens again

Will's next film, in 1997, was *Men in Black*. He played Agent J. Agent J was a **cocky** newcomer to a secret police force. Once again, Will did battle with aliens and came out on top. The combination of Will's sense of humour and the film's amazing special effects made *Men in Black* a classic.

Will learned a lot about acting from his co-star Tommy Lee Jones.

Steven Spielberg asked Will to appear in *Men in Black*.

Tough guys

Will learned a lot about comic acting from his **co-stars** in *Men in Black*, Tommy Lee Jones and Rip Torn. Both actors usually play tough, **gritty** roles. Will was amazed to see how funny they could both be while still being 'tough guys'.

Star words   cocky confident and boastful

Men in Black combined comedy and amazing special effects.

Bad choice?

Like most stars, Will turns down a lot of film offers. There are many reasons why he will not do a film. Sometimes, it is just a 'feeling'. He got that feeling when he read the script for *The Matrix*. He turned down the part of Neo. Keanu Reeves took the part instead and the film became a huge hit. Well, no one is perfect!

Change of direction

Will liked the script for *Men in Black* when he read it. However, he had just made *Independence Day* and he did not want to make another film about aliens. Steven Spielberg was the film's executive **producer**. He had to try hard to make Will play the **role**. How could Will say no? Spielberg had made some of the most successful films ever. These include *Jaws*, *E.T.*, *Raiders of the Lost Ark* and *Jurassic Park*.

Will turned down the lead role in *The Matrix*.

gritty tough and determined

Back to music

★ ★ ★ ★ ★ ★ ★ ★ ★ ★ ★

Rhyme time

How long does it take to write a rap hit? In Will's case, anywhere from five minutes to five months. Sometimes the words just pop into his head. If not, Will just comes back to it again and again until he gets it right.

DJ Jazzy Jeff and the Fresh Prince made their last album, *Code Red*, in 1993. Will was busy with his acting. Jeff Townes started his own record label. Other rap artists were getting more attention anyway. Will disappeared from the music scene for four years.

Return to form

In 1997, Will had a success with the title song for *Men in Black*. This got Will into writing music again. When Will made the video for the song 'Men in black', there were no limits to what it could look like. For the first time, he had a Hollywood film crew, an experienced **director**, and a **big budget** for special effects. The video features a line dance with aliens. It is a classic moment in music video. Will says that the 'Men in black' video was a major event in his life. It gave him freedom to explore new ideas.

Solo album

After this, Will decided to return to the studio and make a solo album. Jeff Townes produced some of the songs. 'Big Willie style' was a huge seller. Another song, 'Gettin' jiggy with it' got to number one on the US singles' chart.

Will made his musical comeback with the *Men in Black* title song.

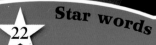
Star words   director person in charge of making a film

New moves

Will's musical success continued in 1999. He made the title song for the film *Wild, Wild West*. He was learning a lot of new dance moves and showing them off in his videos. The music, **lyrics** and images in Will's new works showed a more mature artist. There was still plenty of the **wise-cracking** kid, though. Will released more albums, *Willennium* in 1999, *Born to Reign* in 2002, and *Lost and Found* in 2005. His *Greatest Hits* album came out in 2002, too.

Will puts a lot of energy into his live performances.

Getting jiggy

When *Big Willie Style* came out, everyone wanted to know what 'jiggy' meant. Will says it means a level 'beyond cool'.

Will promoted the release of his album *Willennium* with a live show in Times Square, New York.

lyrics words to a song

Crossing over

People in show business often talk about 'cross-over' appeal. This is when an artist attracts two different groups of fans. Will's first cross-over success came when he began selling records to music fans who had never listened to rap before.

Screen gems

Will's next cross-over **triumph** was *The Fresh Prince of Bel Air*. Millions of people who had never heard his music became fans of Will the actor. Finally, Will made the cross-over from television to films. He gained millions of fans who had never watched his television show.

★ ★ ★ ★ ★ ★ ★ ★ ★ ★ ★

Billion-dollar star

Will's films brought in almost a billion US dollars during the 1990s. His films are watched by millions of fans. He has also won awards for his acting.

★ ★ ★ ★ ★ ★ ★ ★ ★ ★

Not many people have been both a rapper and a sitcom star, like Will has!

Star words   triumph success

Will has won
Grammy awards
both as a solo
artist and as a
duo with Jeff
Townes.

Winning awards

Will has won the top
three awards in
music: the **Grammy**,
American Music
Award and MTV
Music Video Award.
He was **nominated**
for a Golden Globe
as a television actor.
A later triumph for
Will came at the
2002 Academy
Awards. He was
nominated for an
Oscar as Best Actor
in the film *Ali*.

Top dog

Other entertainers have made records, appeared
on television and acted in films, but no one else in
Will's generation has reached the top in all three
areas. It is hard to think of anyone who has
earned the kind of praise he has in music, films
and television. He has had **phenomenal** success.

Team player

Will says he is successful in each because he is
willing to take risks. He opens his mind to new
ideas. He never thinks he knows everything. That
not only makes Will good at what he does, it
makes him a joy to work with.

phenomenal amazing

Ali

Playing a hero

Will worked very hard to play Muhammad Ali. The part was very important to him as Muhammad is one of Will's heroes. Muhammad stood up for his beliefs at a time when African Americans were expected to keep a low profile. Muhammad also showed that an athlete could make a difference.

Will's film **roles** during the 1990s had one thing in common: there was a lot of Will in all of them. That is because **directors** wanted his personality to shine through. That changed when he was offered the role of Muhammad Ali in the 2001 film *Ali*. Muhammad Ali was a boxing champion in the 1960s and 1970s. He was also an important African American. He spoke out against **racism** and stood up for the rights of black people.

Becoming the champion

Will had to change himself completely to play Ali. Will had to copy Muhammad's voice, his movements and his facial expressions.

Muhammad Ali in action. Will worked hard to prepare to play Ali.

Star words

impersonate pretend to be another person by looking and sounding like them

Will in a scene from *Ali*.

★ Star fact

Will nearly turned down the role of Muhammad Ali. He only accepted when Muhammad Ali himself asked him to play the part.

Fit for film

Will has had to stay in top shape for all of his roles, not just for *Ali*. It takes strength and **stamina** to be an actor. If Will gets tired and loses his concentration, then his performance will suffer. Will works out regularly to keep his body and mind strong. All the work Will did for *Ali* paid off when he was **nominated** for an Academy Award.

After months of practice, Will was able to do a good **impersonation**. The biggest challenge was to make himself look like a professional boxer. Will is fit and well built, but he does not have a boxer's **physique**. There was no way to fake this. Will had to work hard to change his body.

Working out

Will went to the gym for months to do workouts. Slowly but surely, he began to put on muscle. He also had to learn how to punch and move like a boxer. He weighed more than 91 kilograms when filming began.

Will and his wife Jada on Oscar night 2002.

stamina ability to be active for a long time
physique body

Public and private

What's it worth?

Collecting Will Smith memorabilia is a passion for thousands of his fans. An online search turned up these items:

Men in Black keyring... US#5

Independence Day trading card set...US#15

Wild, Wild West film poster...US#20

Signed photo of Will...US#50

Will has had hit records, a hit television show, and starred in **blockbuster** films. He has fans all over the world. Everywhere he goes he is met by admirers, asking for autographs. At times they invade his privacy. Will understands that this is part of being a celebrity. He tries to be nice to his fans at all times, even when he does not feel like it.

Staying loose

Some of Will's biggest fans are the people he has worked with. He is friendly to crew members when he makes films. He is also a big practical joker. When Will is around, you never know what will happen next!

Will takes time to sign autographs for his fans.

Star words   memorabilia valuable objects from an event, film or television programme or famous person's life

Here, Will is
promoting
the film *Wild,
Wild West*.

Serious side

Actors and musicians who have worked with
Will praise him for his hard work. **Directors**
admire the way he puts himself into his parts.
Barry Sonnenfeld
directed Will in *Wild,
Wild West* and the
Men in Black films.
He says Will has
much more to achieve
as an actor.

Will's good looks
have helped to
make him a star.

★ ★ ★ ★ ★ ★ ★ ★ ★ ★ ★ ★

Star quality

In 1998 *People*
Magazine put Will
on its list of the
50 most beautiful
people in the world.

★ ★ ★ ★ ★ ★ ★ ★ ★ ★ ★ ★

A fresh start

Will was foolish with his money when he was young. Luckily, *The Fresh Prince* was a hit series. This meant Will was able to pay the government the taxes he owed. Since then Will has been very careful with his money.

Hard lessons

Being talented and hard-working can make you rich and famous. Being rich and famous does not make you wise, however. Will learned this lesson twice as a young man. The album *He's the DJ, I'm the Rapper* sold one million copies in 1988. Will became a millionaire many times over when he was just twenty years old. Will and Jeff had more money than they could count. The problem was, they did not keep track of how much money they were spending.

Will and Jeff together in 1990. They were soon to run into money troubles.

Star words   lavish wealthy and luxurious

Easy come, easy go

Will bought anything that caught his eye. He did not care how much it cost. He had a **lavish** lifestyle. He took his friends on expensive holidays. When DJ Jazzy Jeff and The Fresh Prince went on tour, they spent more money than they were making. They ate in the best restaurants. They rode in limousines. They took private jets whenever they travelled. In 1990, the government told Will that he owed millions of dollars in **income tax**. The bill was more than he had in the bank. He was broke!

Will and Jeff led a life of luxury, being driven around in expensive cars.

Will with his first wife, Sheree Zampino.

Failure

When Will first started acting, he took his work problems home. When he made *Six Degrees of Separation*, he got very wrapped up in his character. This had a bad effect on his marriage and it began to fall apart. He and Sheree were divorced in 1995. Will considers this his biggest failure. Now he knows where to draw the line between work and family life.

income tax money you pay to the government each year, based on what you earn

Getting it right

Will began going out with actress Jada Pinkett after his divorce in 1995. Jada's career was also taking off. She understood how hard actors have to work. She also knew how the pressures of show business could hurt a marriage.

Making a plan

Will and Jada agreed on a plan for working out the problems actors have in relationships. They married on New Year's Eve in 1997. They were determined to keep the event private. They picked up their guests in limousines and drove them to a secret location.

Making it work

Some celebrity couples seem happy together, like Tim Robbins and Susan Sarandon (above), or Brad Pitt and Jennifer Aniston. Show business marriages often break down, though. There is a lot of pressure on them.

Will's wife Jada strikes a pose.

Jada starred in *The Nutty Professor* with Eddie Murphy.

Class act

Among the films Jada has made are:
The Matrix Revolutions (2003)
The Matrix Reloaded (2003)
Ali (2001)
Bamboozled (2000)
Return to Paradise (1998)
Scream 2 (1997)
Set It Off (1996)
The Nutty Professor (1996).

Power couple

Will and Jada are one of Hollywood's most admired couples. They seem to have succeeded where many others have failed. They try to get the right mix of work and family time. A lot of Hollywood marriages fail, but Will and Jada might just stay together.

Will's family

Will and Jada have two children together. Their son is called Jaden Christopher Syre. He was born on 8 July 1998. Their daughter is called Willow Camille Reign. She was born on 31 October 2000.

★ Star fact

Will met both his wives on the **sets** of television shows. He met Sheree when he was visiting a friend at *A Different World*. He met Jada on the *Fresh Prince* set.

Balancing act

Balancing work and family time is a challenge for anyone. For Will, it has been very difficult. Will's first marriage broke up because he was unable to find this balance. Now he is much better at dividing his time between his many projects and his wife and children.

Always busy

Will hates it when he has nothing to do. This means that he often takes on more than he can handle. Will does not like to let others do his work. He is a **perfectionist**. This has made him a **workaholic**.

Will and Jada are often seen out at film premieres.

★ ★ ★ ★ ★ ★ ★ ★ ★ ★

Where's Will?

Will keeps his private life private. Where is the best place to spot the Smiths in public? Your best chance is at film **premieres**.

★ ★ ★ ★ ★ ★ ★ ★ ★ ★

Near and dear

The thing that drives Will to succeed in his career threatens to take him away from the people he loves. He has tried to make sure this does not happen. Will built a recording studio and business office in his home. This means that he can work hard without being far from his family. That also means more quality time with Jada, Trey, Jaden and Willow. He has become a good husband and father.

> A man and a woman together, raising a family, is the purest form of happiness we can experience.

Star words   premiere first showing of a film, often with celebrities invited

Music fan

Will is a big fan of other rap artists. Some of his favourites are LL Cool J, Biggie Small and The Fugees (left). He also likes to keep up with new artists.

Will's parents

Will says his parents helped him to be a better husband and father. He passes on the lessons they taught him as a child to his own children.

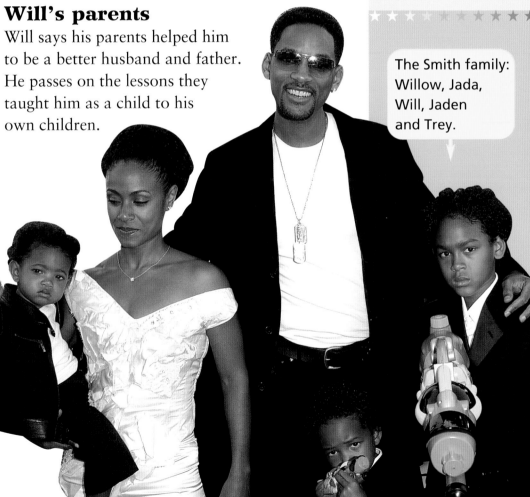

The Smith family: Willow, Jada, Will, Jaden and Trey.

perfectionist someone who wants to do everything perfectly
workaholic someone who loves working

Style and image

What's in the wardrobe?

Will loves to show himself off at big Hollywood events. He is at his best when he is on the red carpet.

Image means a lot in show business. Will has known this since he was a teenager. He is always thinking about how he looks and acts in public. He is careful about what he says. Is it a hassle? Yes, sometimes it is. Will believes it is worth the extra effort, though. He has high standards for himself. He knows that he must meet those standards every time he steps out in public.

Fresh style

On *The Fresh Prince of Bel Air*, Will wore cool and colourful hip-hop clothing. His cousin Carlton looked much smarter and more uptight. This was the source of some great jokes.

Cool couple

Will has gone from being a hip-hop fashion icon to one of the coolest dressers in Hollywood. He has learned how to make a smooth entrance at industry events such as film **premieres**. Of course, it helps to have Jada by his side.

Will and Jada looking cool and casual.

Star words image way someone looks and dresses

Will shows off his unique sense of style.

Model citizen

Will is a favourite of the fashion world. He is tall, well-built and graceful. Will looks great in expensive designer suits (below). He also makes casual clothes look good.

★ ★ ★ ★ ★ ★ ★ ★ ★ ★

★ Star fact

A woman once saw Will on the street and was so excited she crashed her car. Instead of worrying about the damage, she ran over and asked for his autograph.

Now and then

In the swim

Will learned about **animation** and **voice-over** work in 2004. He played the lead role in an animated film called *Shark Tale*. Do not be surprised if Will makes an animated film himself one day.

Will is naturally curious and wants to learn. He likes talking to other actors and musicians. Will also enjoys watching how people behind the scenes work, like the people who operate cameras. He is always picking up tips from **producers** and **directors**. It was only a matter of time before he formed his own company.

The company

Will's company is called Overbrook Entertainment. It was named after Will's old school in Philadelphia. The company has several projects lined up.

Will has spent a lot of time on film **sets**. Is it time for him to get behind the camera?

Star words   animation making a film using drawings, puppets or computer graphics instead of actors

Will and Jada wrote a script for a film called *Love for Hire*. They hope it will become a hit. In 2003, they produced a television comedy called *All of Us*.

Behind the camera

Will is certain he will be working 'behind the camera' in the future. He has been learning the business for more than ten years. He also has good attention to detail and works well with other people. Will's ability to organize and plan will help him if he becomes a producer. A producer sees to all the details of film-making and pays all the bills.

Will's good friend Denzel Washington directed a film called *Antwone Fisher*.

Actors turned directors

If Will becomes a director, he will not be the first performer to do so. Sofia Coppola, Robert Redford, Woody Allen, Denzel Washington, Kevin Costner, Jodie Foster and Clint Eastwood all received great reviews for their work as directors.

Mel Gibson is another Hollywood star who has become a director.

voice-over voice given to a cartoon character

Past and present

Will's friends and family say he is still the same sweet person they knew as a teenager in Philadelphia. The changes fans have seen are mostly on the outside. What you see today is partly the result of growing up. But those changes have been important to Will's career.

Will first became known as a streetwise, funny rapper.

Risky business

Every time celebrities change their **image**, they take a big risk. What if old fans feel they do not know you anymore? What if they no longer find you interesting?

Keeping it real

Will became famous as a young rapper. He changed his look to a **wise-cracking** teenager for his television character. When Will began starring in films, he had to be tough and sophisticated. How did Will make these changes without losing his fans? His sense of humour still came through. This is what people connect with.

★ ★ ★ ★ ★ ★ ★ ★ ★ ★

Back to TV

Will returned to television in 2003. He was a guest star on the US comedy series he and Jada produce: *All of Us*. He rapped '80s style' on the programme.

★ ★ ★ ★ ★ ★ ★ ★ ★ ★

Star words caddy person who carries a golf player's clubs

Higher power

Will always joked that the film role he most wanted to play was God. In *The Legend of Bagger Vance*, he got the chance. Will plays a golf **caddy** who magically appears to help a young man put his life back together. Director Robert Redford told Will that the character of Bagger represented a 'higher power'.

Will has matured but he has stayed true to his roots.

Up ahead

It will be interesting to see what lies ahead for Will. If he becomes a **producer** or a **director**, will the qualities that made him a star also make fans want to see his films?

Will with Matt Damon and Charlize Theron in *The Legend of Bagger Vance*.

Eureka!

Will turned down a **scholarship** to the Massachusetts Institute of Technology (MIT) to become a rapper instead. MIT is one of the top centres of learning in the world.

Where there's a will...

Whoever said 'where there's a will there's a way' must have had someone like Will in mind. When Will sets his mind on something, he does whatever it takes to reach that goal. Will has focus, determination, confidence and **charisma**. He never stops pushing himself and exploring his talent.

Street smart

Will is a dreamer. But he also knows that dreams do not come true unless you are willing to take action. He is organized and pays attention to details.

> " People laugh, but if I set my mind to it, within the next 15 years I would be president. "

Agent J and Agent K back for *Men in Black II*.

Star words   scholarship offer for a free education

He really listens to people when they talk, and he is not afraid to ask questions. Looking back, this is what took Will from the street parties of Philadelphia to the top of the entertainment business. Looking ahead, these qualities should take him as far as he wants to go.

Recent work

Among Will's recent successes are two sequels: *Men in Black II* and *Bad Boys II*. Fans **flocked** to cinemas and video stores to see Will reunited with Tommy Lee Jones and Martin Lawrence.

There will be more amazing live shows from Will.

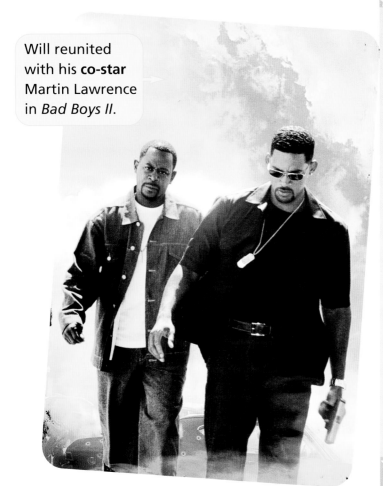

Will reunited with his **co-star** Martin Lawrence in *Bad Boys II*.

Dreaming big

It is hard to say where Will's dreams will take him. He has a new contract with Columbia Records, which means he will be working hard in the studio to make new music. Fans can hardly wait for his next album. Of course, he is always working on a new film. Will thinks about new projects all the time. When he puts his mind to something, nothing can stop him.

flock go in large numbers

Books

Just the Two of Us, Will Smith
   (Scholastic, 2000)
Will Power!, Jan Berenson
   (Simon & Schuster, 1997)
Will Smith, Meg Greene
   (Chelsea House, 2001)
Will Smith, Stacey Stauffer
   (Chelsea House, 1999)
Will Smith: The Freshest Prince, Mark Bego
   (Andrews McMeel, 1998)
*Will Smith: From Fresh Prince to King of
   Cool*, K.S. Rodriguez (HarperCollins, 1998)

Filmography

The Pursuit of Happiness (due 2006)
Tonight, He Comes (due 2006)
Hitch (2005)
Shark Tale (2004)
I, Robot (2004)
Bad Boys II (2003)
Men in Black II (2002)
Ali (2001)
The Legend of Bagger Vance (2000)
Wild, Wild West (1999)
Enemy of the State (1998)
Men in Black (1997)
Independence Day (1996)
Bad Boys (1995)
Six Degrees of Separation (1994)
Made in America (1993)

Where the Day Takes You (1992)
The Imagemaker (1986)

Television
The Fresh Prince of Bel Air (1990–96)

Discography
Lost and Found (2005)
Greatest Hits (2002)
Born to Reign (2002)
Willennium (1999)
Big Willie Style (1997)
Code Red (1993) DJ Jazzy Jeff and the
    Fresh Prince
Home Base (1991) DJ Jazzy Jeff and the
    Fresh Prince
He's the DJ, I'm the Rapper (1988) DJ Jazzy
    Jeff and the Fresh Prince
Rock the House (1987) DJ Jazzy Jeff and the
    Fresh Prince

Websites
Many of Will's fans log on to websites for the
latest information. Some of the best are:
http://www.willsmith.com
http://www.mtv.com
http://www.bbc.co.uk/totp

Disclaimer
All the Internet addresses (URLs) given in this book were valid at the
time of going to press. However, due to the dynamic nature of the
Internet, some addresses may have changed, or sites may have ceased
to exist since publication. While the author and publishers regret any
inconvenience this may cause readers, no responsibility for any such
changes can be accepted by either the author or the publishers.

Glossary

administrator someone who helps to run a school, business or other organization

animation making a film using drawings, puppets or computer graphics instead of actors

anxiety worry

audition interview for a musician or actor, where they show their skills

big budget large amount of money available to spend. A big budget film is made using a lot of money.

blockbuster successful big budget film

caddy person who carries a golf player's clubs

charisma charm and appeal

cocky confident and boastful

con man someone who wins the trust of others, then steals from them

co-stars actors appearing together in a film or television show

director person in charge of making a film

flock go in large numbers

foster family when children cannot live with their own parents they may live for a while with another family. This is their foster family.

Grammy award given at America's most important annual popular music industry awards

gritty tough and determined

hardships difficulties and challenges

image way someone looks and dresses

impersonate pretend to be another person by looking and sounding like them

income tax money you pay to the government each year, based on what you earn

injustice unfairness

inspire give someone the idea or motivation to do something

lavish wealthy and luxurious

low budget small amount of money available to spend. A low budget film does not cost much money to make.

lyrics words to a song

memorabilia valuable objects from an event, film or television programme or famous person's life

nominated to be put forward as one of the people to win an award

orphan someone whose parents are dead

perfectionist someone who wants to do everything perfectly

phenomenal amazing

physique body

premiere first showing of a film, often with celebrities invited

producer person in charge of making a record, film or television show

professional someone who does their job very well

racism when people are treated unfairly because of their race or the colour of their skin

role part that an actor plays in a film, play or television show

scholarship offer for a free education

set part of a film studio where a film is shot

silver screen nickname for the large screen at the cinema

stamina ability to be active for a long time

triumph success

voice-over voice given to a cartoon character

wise-cracking making a lot of jokes

witness someone who has seen a crime take place

workaholic someone who loves working

Index